If you do not have a personal relationship with Jesus Christ, I encourage you today to do so. Repent and believe that Jesus died on the cross for your sins and took your punishment upon Himself, was buried and on the third day rose from the grave. If you give your life to Jesus by accepting what He did for you, He will give you eternal life. Call on Jesus Christ today for the salvation of your soul.

16 For God so loved the world that He gave His one and only Son, that everyone who believes in Him shall not perish but have eternal life. 17 For God did not send His Son into the world to condemn the world, but to save the world through Him. 18 Whoever believes in Him is not condemned, but whoever does not believe has already been condemned, because he has not believed in the name of God's one and only Son. **-John 3:16-18 BSB**

Pray this prayer if you want to follow Jesus today and be forgiven of all your sins

Make these words your own

Father in heaven, in the name of the Lord Jesus Christ. I confess Lord that I'm a sinner and only through You Lord Jesus can my sins be forgiven. I believe that You died for my sins on the cross and on the third day You rose from the grave. Forgive me for all the bad things I have done and save me today. I want to follow You for the rest of my life so that I may do Your will, In Jesus' name I pray, Amen.

Cover by Seth V. Arao
Commentary by Alex Ruiz

Ministry
Websites: Spiritualminefield.wordpress.com
Spiritualminefield.com
thecookieadaysite.wordpress.com

The Holy Bible, Berean Study Bible, BSB
Copyright ©2016, 2020 by Bible Hub
Used by Permission. All Rights Reserved Worldwide.

Copyright © 2021 Alex Ruiz
All rights reserved.

No part of the commentary in this book may be reproduced in any form without written permission from the author. You may quote from the commentary for a bible study without changing any wording of this commentary.

978-1-387-89305-8
Lulu.com

Spiritual Warfare
A look into the spiritual realm

The Table of Contents

The Full Armor Of God

An Introduction..........Page 1

The Belt of Truth..........Page 4

The Breastplate of Righteousness..........Page 7

Feet Fitted (Shoes)..........Page 10

The Shield of Faith..........Page 13

The Helmet of Salvation..........Page 15

The Sword (The Word of God)..........Page 18

Looking into The Sinister Structure of Satan and His Fallen Angels..........Page 20

Part 1
Demons and The Tactics They Use to Entrap You..........Page 25

Part 2
Demons and The Tactics They Use to Entrap You..........Page 32

What is Demonic Oppression?..........Page 35

Can a Christian be Possessed by a Demon?..........Page 41

Demons are Like Ninjas..........Page 44

Why Satan Wants You to Doubt The Bible..........Page 47

The Demon of Flattery..........Page 51

Satan's Lie: You Can Become Like God..........Page 54

Satan is Like a Shark..........Page 59

The True Virus "The Devil"..........Page 62

How Well are You Protected from Deception?..........Page 65

Satan's Three Steps to Deception..........Page 68

The End Times

Which Death Do You Prefer?..........Page 71

What Does The Number 666 mean?..........Page 73

The End Times Apostasy..........Page 77

A Worldwide Collapse Will Introduce The Mark of The Beast..........Page 80

Salvation

Salvation is only through faith in Jesus Christ..........Page 83

Note Taking

Notes..........Pages 88-91

The Full Armor Of God
An introduction

"10 Finally, be strong in the Lord and in His mighty power. 11 Put on the full armor of God, so that you can make your stand against the devil's schemes. 12 For our struggle is not against flesh and blood, but against the rulers, against the authorities, against the powers of this world's darkness, and against the spiritual forces of evil in the heavenly realms. 13 Therefore take up the full armor of God, so that when the day of evil comes, you will be able to stand your ground, and having done everything, to stand." **-Ephesians 6:10-13 BSB**

Before a soldier goes to battle, he equips himself with gear that will protect him and with weapons to use on the battlefield to defeat his enemy. As Christians, it is essential to armor up with the Armor of God to fight—not men and women, but something much more sinister, deceptive, and dark—a hater of anything good and a murderer, which is Satan, and his demonic forces. This is what the believers in Christ are up against.

What is the Full Armor of God, and how exactly do we put it on? To put it on is by first of all being a follower of Jesus Christ and then living a life of righteousness in obedience to the Word of God and not living a life that the world lives according to **Romans 13:12-13**.

"12 The night is nearly over; the day has drawn near. So let us lay aside the deeds of darkness and put on the armor of light. 13 Let us behave decently, as in the daytime, not in carousing and drunkenness, not in sexual immorality and debauchery, not in dissension and jealousy." **-Romans 13:12-13 BSB**

The Full Armor of God Represents Jesus Christ

"Instead, clothe yourselves with the Lord Jesus Christ, and make no provision for the desires of the flesh." **-Romans 13:14 BSB**

Christians who rely only on the Lord Jesus Christ by living according to the Scriptures will be equipped with the Full Armor of God because the Lord will be their protector so that they won't be defeated by the enemy. A Christian gets defeated by taking it off, which occurs when they are living in sin. Jesus will not protect a child in disobedience, but would allow for their defeat to take place so that they will come to repentance. Without the Armor, we are nothing, but with it, we are victorious in Jesus Christ, so remember that as believers, our lifeline is to:

1. Pray to the Lord with thanksgiving for everything He has done for us and ask Him for strength to do His will and to be protected against the evil one.
2. Read the Bible daily so that our minds may be filled with God's Word and our desires may be transformed into what God desires, which will keep us from stumbling (**Psalms 119:9,11**).
3. And third, let the Word of God transform us so we may live lives that will please the Lord and will equip us to defend the Bible, protect ourselves from false doctrine, and not only have answers for people's questions but to tell them the good news about Jesus' death and resurrection.

4.

THE FULL ARMOR OF GOD
THE BELT OF TRUTH

5.

Stand firm then, with **the belt of truth** buckled around your waist,... -**Ephesians 6:14(a) BSB**

A soldier's belt is very important because it holds the sword and his pants in place. Even though it might seem less vital than the sword and shield, without it you cannot go into battle because you would lose your weapon while heading towards the battlefield, which would be quite catastrophic. What is the truth (belt)? **John 14:6** states, "Jesus answered, "I am the way and the truth and the life. No one comes to the Father except through Me."

Truth is the reality of how things are and what's real, and Jesus clearly stated that without faith in Him, there is no way ANY person can go to the Father. If anyone tells you that all roads (all religion) lead you to God, that is none other than a blatant LIE. Imagine being in the wilderness, and it's nearing nightfall. You see yourself lost, and you frantically search for your compass to navigate through this hostile place, not knowing that the imitation compass you relied on was cheaply made.

It malfunctions because you did not want to get the tried and true brand name compass. You want to go north, but the malfunctioning cheap compass is sending you south, deeper into the wilderness, which makes your chances of survival minuscule, thinking that the compass is leading you in the right direction.

This is how it is when you follow or believe something or someone and not the Bible (The truth). We need to be grounded in God's Word, which is a lamp to our feet that lights up our path to find how we should go (to do God's will), and also, we won't fall into a ditch (false doctrine). Without truth, you won't follow the right Jesus, and you would end up following the Jesus of the Quran, Mormonism, or any other Jesus that they claim is not God.

In **John 8:24**, Jesus said, "That is why I told you that you would die in your sins. For unless you believe that I am He, you will die in your sins."

Without truth, there is no salvation because it will lead you to the wrong Jesus, who is NOT the savior. The truth can only be known if one goes to the Word of God, which is God-breathed. Those who love God's Word show that they love Jesus because He is Truth and His Word is truth for the glory of God the Father. By reading it every day, you will grow up in maturity and the image of God the Son, and you will have the Belt of Truth around your waist to carry your weapon so you won't be caught off guard by the enemy, the forces of darkness.

The Full Armor of God
the breastplate of righteousness

8.

...with the **breastplate of righteousness** arrayed, -Ephesians 6:14(b) BSB

The breastplate protects the heart, stomach, liver, and all the other vital organs of the soldier. When a person puts their trust and faith in Jesus Christ as Lord and Savior, Jesus' righteousness gets credited (**2 Corinthians 5:21**) into the person's account, as if they lived Jesus' life, and the person gets the breastplate of righteousness.

Now that the Lord gave us the breastplate, we must wear it every day, especially since we are always on the battlefield. We wear the breastplate by living a life of obedience to the Word of God. We must always be ready, for the enemy is consistently on the lookout to see if we have the Armor of God on or if there's a piece of the Armor we don't have on. In a real battle, the enemy will wait patiently to catch us off guard and aim at the unprotected body part. In this case, let's say you are not wearing your breastplate, which is one of the most important pieces of armor you could have. If an arrow hits you in one of your major organs, like the heart, that will be a kill shot.

The arrows of Satan are deception, and your heart is the core of your feelings. The enemy will attack your feelings to draw you away from the Lord by falling in love with a woman who is not a Christian (this happened to King Solomon, **1 Kings 11:4**), give you "good" friends who will take you away from the Lord, or a job that makes you do things that go against the Scriptures. These are some of the reasons why we cannot be driven by our emotions because they can be dangerous and deceptive. We must be driven by the Word of God, for it will always lead us into all righteousness and teach us the way to please the Lord and to do His will.

9.

"7 But blessed is the man who trusts in the LORD, whose confidence is in Him. 8 He is like a tree planted by the waters that sends out its roots toward the stream. It does not fear when the heat comes, and its leaves are always green. It does not worry in a year of drought, nor does it cease to produce fruit. 9 The heart is deceitful above all things and beyond cure. Who can understand it?" **-Jeremiah 17:7-9 BSB**

10.

The Full Armor Of God
Feet Fitted (shoes)

and with your **feet fitted** with the readiness of **the gospel of peace**. -**Ephesians 6:15 BSB**

The soldier's shoes had spikes underneath them to keep them from losing their footing while fighting their enemies, who would plant oil and anything else on the ground to make them slip and get hurt, disabling them from participating in the battle. We see this with anything that diverts our attention from preaching the gospel. We become spiritually desensitized, which will keep us from completing the work that God gave us to do until we have drifted dangerously far from God and become incapacitated, unable to be used by Him. With the gospel on our feet, it will keep us grounded in the Scriptures without deviating from our task. The Holy Spirit will guide us to those who need to hear the good news, like one suffering from an illness, or depression, family problems, or any other given situation they are going through. As you bring them the good news of Jesus Christ, you give them hope.

"The light of the eyes cheers the heart, and good news nourishes the bones." -**Proverbs 15:30 BSB**

"How beautiful on the mountains are the feet of those who bring good news, who proclaim peace, who bring good tidings, who proclaim salvation, who say to Zion, "Your God reigns!" -**Isaiah 52:7 BSB**

Jesus commanded us in **Matthew 28:19-20**, "Therefore go and make disciples of all nations, baptizing them in the name of the Father, and of the Son, and of the Holy Spirit, 20 and teaching them to obey all that I have commanded you. And surely I am with you always, even to the end of the age."

12.

We must be obedient to the Lord by telling people about this wonderful gospel that will save them from a literal hell. Not telling people about Jesus equates to wanting them to go to hell. If you are a believer, remember that Jesus, in His great mercy, sent someone to tell you about Him, so you, in turn, are expected to do the same for someone else. Loving Jesus is expressed by keeping His Word and loving your neighbor as yourself.

The Full Armor Of God
THE SHIELD OF FAITH

14.

In addition to all this, take up **the shield of faith**, with which you can extinguish all the flaming arrows of the evil one. -**Ephesians 6:16 BSB**

The shield that Paul was probably referring to was a Roman shield called Scutum. It was rectangular with a semi-round shape to reflect arrows from the front and sides to protect the soldier as much as possible. The arrows from the enemy come in all sizes, purposely doused with tar, which keeps the fire on the arrow lit while in the air to do maximum damage when it hits. Without faith, it is impossible to please God (**Hebrews 11:6**). We must continue to trust the Lord and keep the faith regardless of our circumstances because Satan desires for us to curse God (**Job 1:11**), to abandon our faith in the Lord Jesus Christ. Without the shield of faith, the flaming arrows would hit your armor and splatter fire all over you, causing you to drop your sword to put out the fire, making you vulnerable and susceptible to a kill shot.

When someone doubts the Lord's faithfulness, especially when going through extreme circumstances, and the person feels as if God has abandoned them, that person has dropped their shield and is in grave danger of having their faith hit by another flaming arrow. If that arrow is anger, spiritually speaking, it will eventually turn into bitterness and from bitterness to desperation and from desperation to ungodly behavior, then finally cursing God (abandoning the faith). Jesus said in **Luke 18:1**, "Then Jesus told them a parable about their need to pray at all times and not lose heart."

No matter what happens, keep the faith, for in doing so you will reap the benefit that the Lord has in store for you and will bring Him glory. He will never leave you nor forsake you.

The Full Armor Of God
THE HELMET OF SALVATION

16.

And take **the helmet of salvation**... -Ephesians 6:17(a) BSB

The helmet in Latin is called a Galea, which resembles a calyx. The calyx is a leaf-like structure that engulfs a flower while it is developing. Its purpose is to protect it from drying out and dying. In the same way, when a person puts their faith and trust in Jesus as Lord and Savior, one of the first pieces of armor given to him is the helmet of salvation, which protects his mind while he is developing into a mature believer in Jesus Christ. The helmet is an essential piece of armor that a person can have because, without it, one blow to the head from the enemy could lead to spiritual death.

The blows from the demonic forces to your head would be false doctrines, lust, and hopelessness that lead one to curse God in times of difficulty. However, one of the hardest hits from the enemy is when you start to doubt your salvation in the Lord Jesus. If you have the helmet as you depend on the Lord, the spiritual damage is minimal. Imagine not having the helmet on and being unprotected. Satan will attack you with thoughts of not being saved —that God has abandoned you—and it will destroy you instantly. The "believer" will succumb to the lie and stop following Christ.

A genuine believer will never lose his or her salvation (**John 10:28**). If one does walk away from Jesus Christ, it proves that they were never saved in the first place (**1 John 2:19**).

- "I give them eternal life, and they will never perish. No one can snatch them out of My hand." **-John 10:28 BSB**
- "They went out from us, but they did not belong to us. For if they had belonged to us, they would have remained with us. But their departure made it clear that none of them belonged to us." **-1 John 2:19 BSB**

17.

If anyone ever tells you that you are not saved, that statement comes from Satan as an attack on your mind. It is imperative to have your helmet of salvation on by remembering what the Scripture promises, like in the Book of **John 10:28**. Do not believe the Satan's lie because his very intent is to accuse you before God, as found in **Revelation 12:10**, which says, "And I heard a loud voice in heaven saying: "Now have come the salvation and the power and the kingdom of our God, and the authority of His Christ. For the accuser of our brothers has been thrown down—he who accuses them day and night before our God."

If you are living a lifestyle of sin, never repenting or having any remorse over it, and you are not seeking the Lord through His Word or prayer, then take it as a cue that the Lord is telling you to get saved—putting your faith and trust in the Lord Jesus Christ—so that you may live a life of holiness, righteousness, and participating in His will.

The battlefield is in the mind of the believer. Your mind must always be protected by putting on Christ through the obedience of His Word and always repenting of your sins, making sure that you are right in the Lord's eyes by the way you live. Remember, being attacked by demons is not a matter of **if** but **when**. We have to be ready in season and out of season so that we will be alert and not surprised by their hits.

18.

The Full Armor Of God
the sword

19.

...and **the sword** of the Spirit, which is the word of God.
-**Ephesians 6:17(b) BSB**

The Roman sword was called gladius in Latin, and one of the words derived from gladius is gladiator, which means swordsman. It was a two-edged sword used for cutting and had a pointed tip for stabbing the enemy. The person's name was often engraved on the sword. As Christians, we are armed with the sword and must be prepared as a gladiator for battle with no fear because Jesus is the One who fights our battles. The sword we use for the battle is engraved with the phrase "the Word of God", which is a phrase that belongs to Jesus Christ, see **Revelation 19:13**. So when we fight the demonic forces, it is done through an offensive weapon, the sword, to cut and pierce the enemy with the Word of God, which has power and authority.

It is called the sword of the Spirit, which gives us an understanding of what is revealed in Holy Scripture. The more we read and study the word, the better we get at using the sword against the enemy. We are not just to block the enemy's attack through the shield of faith, but we must go into the offense to slash and destroy the enemy with the Word of God. Memorizing Bible verses and using them when the enemy tries to deceive or trap us will help us not sin against the Lord.

Jesus Himself quoted Scripture to attack Satan's temptations (**Matthew 4:3-11**). By using the sword, we are depending on Christ's strength as found in **Ephesians 6:10**, "Finally, be strong in the Lord and in His mighty power." It is important to meditate on God's Word daily because the day of evil will come and try to destroy our faith in Christ Jesus, and a believer must be ready at all times.

20.

Looking into The sinister structure of satan and his fallen angels

As followers of the Lord Jesus Christ, we face daily demonic entities who are always planning their next attack to stop us from accomplishing God's will. Why? Because they hate God and are pure evil. But that's not the only reason. They attack believers so that the gospel doesn't reach others and get them saved. They want people to go to hell and burn for all eternity. Demons will go above and beyond to keep your neighbors, friends, and family from hearing the message that God has given you through the Scriptures. We will get into more details on the demonic forces of evil that we face every day to show you how serious our battles are and the need for us to get closer to the Lord.

"For our struggle is not against flesh and blood, but against the **rulers**, against the **authorities**, against the **powers** of this world's darkness, and against the **spiritual forces of evil** in **the heavenly realms**." -Ephesians 6:12 BSB

The bold and underlined words above will bring to light the structure of the fallen angels and their goal for humanity.

Our fight is against Satan and his fallen angels.

Ephesians 6:12 (*For our struggle is not against flesh and blood*) starts by clarifying that we are not in battle with people, but with what's behind the people who come to either deceive you or harm you. Evil people are under demonic influence to destroy your faith in Christ, and if they can, physically. The good news is that we are under God's protection (**Job 1:10**).

"Have You not placed a hedge on every side around him and his household and all that he owns? You have blessed the work of his hands, and his possessions have increased in the land." **-Job 1:10 BSB**

Rulers: In Greek (*#746*), this word reveals that the demons have a hierarchical structure. You have in their ranks *chief*—head over the rest to command and give strategy to fight against God's people, and *kingly*—who is in charge over a massive demonic army and reveals spiritual power.

Authorities: This word in Greek (*#1849*) shows that they have spiritual power to influence people (**2 Timothy 2:26**) to go against God—rant and blaspheme His name (**Revelation 13:5-6**). They also push people to live in sin—having a strong pull to make people give in to the flesh. These fallen angels have the power to take control of your life (**Luke 22:3-4**). It won't be to make it better but to make your life worse. Believers in Jesus Christ can permit the enemy to cause havoc in their lives by opening up a door (**Ephesians 4:26-27**).

- "Then they will come to their senses and escape the snare of the devil, who has taken them captive to his will." **-2 Timothy 2:26 BSB**

- "5 The beast was given a mouth to speak arrogant and blasphemous words, and authority to act for 42 months. 6 And the beast opened its mouth to speak blasphemies against God and to slander His name and His tabernacle—those who dwell in heaven." **-Revelation 13:5-6 BSB**

- "3 Then Satan entered Judas Iscariot, who was one of the Twelve. 4 And Judas went to discuss with the chief priests and temple officers how he might betray Jesus to them." **-Luke 22:3-4 BSB**

- "26 "Be angry, yet do not sin." Do not let the sun set upon your anger, 27 and do not give the devil a foothold." **-Ephesians 4:26-27 BSB**

Powers: This word in Greek (*#2888*) means that these demonic beings are the rulers of this world (**2 Corinthians 4:4**), who have detached themselves from God during the rebellion of Satan that took place in heaven before men came into existence. They are the ones who infiltrate the world governments (**Daniel 10:13, 20**) to change their policies that will work against God's plan. The ultimate goal is to place the Antichrist in authority to rule the world for Satan (**2 Thessalonians 2:4**).

- "The god of this age has blinded the minds of unbelievers so they cannot see the light of the gospel of the glory of Christ, who is the image of God." **-2 Corinthians 4:4 BSB**
- "13 However, the prince of the kingdom of Persia opposed me for twenty-one days. Then Michael, one of the chief princes, came to help me, for I had been left there with the kings of Persia."...20 "Do you know why I have come to you?" he said. "I must return at once to fight against the prince of Persia, and when I have gone forth, behold, the prince of Greece will come." **-Daniel 10:13, 20 BSB**
- "He will oppose and exalt himself above every so-called god or object of worship. So he will seat himself in the temple of God, proclaiming himself to be God." **-2 Thessalonians 2:4 BSB**

Darkness: This word in Greek (*#4655*) reveals that they want to plunge the world into sin—moral decay. When a person is in the flesh—feeding its desires—they are in darkness walking with a blindfold in the direction of a spiritual cliff.

Spiritual Forces: This word in Greek (*#4152*) indicates that we are in a spiritual battle as the enemies we face are spiritual beings. They operate in the spiritual realm, which manifests in the physical world. So, before a satanic attack happens in the physical world, it first occurs in the spiritual. When a false religious group (i.e., Mormons or Jehovah's Witnesses) comes knocking at your door, the plan of deception was already hatched in the spiritual world to send them to you for entrapment—a spiritual net.

Evil: This word (*Gr. #4188*) shows you the enemy's nature and desires for the human race. It gives you the words wickedness, iniquities, with pain. All this means that the demons, through a sinful lifestyle, will bring you extreme mental and physical pain. This demonic strategy is to get you so tired of life that you would commit suicide—sending you straight to hell for the ultimate torment (**Matthew 27:1-5**).

"When morning came, all the chief priests and elders of the people conspired against Jesus to put Him to death. 2 They bound Him, led Him away, and handed Him over to Pilate the governor. 3 When Judas, who had betrayed Him, saw that Jesus was condemned, he was filled with remorse and returned the thirty pieces of silver to the chief priests and elders. 4 "I have sinned by betraying innocent blood," he said. "What is that to us?" they replied. "You bear the responsibility." 5 So Judas threw the silver into the temple and left. Then he went away and hanged himself."
-Matthew 27:1-5 BSB

Heavenly Realms: This Greek word (*#2032*) means that all angelic activities happen in the spiritual world. It is where God instructs His angels to do His will and where the demons and God's angels fight. Through the spiritual realm, they influence certain situations to impact people's lives.

PART 1: DEMONS AND THE TACTICS
THEY USE TO ENTRAP YOU

26.

Demons are always, in the ready, to battle against the believers to make them weak and unable to do God's will.

Fallen angels (i.e., demons) are those who have abandoned their position and rebelled against the LORD in heaven to follow Satan due to him deceiving them.

"3 Then another sign appeared in heaven: a huge red dragon with seven heads, ten horns, and seven royal crowns on his heads. 4 His tail swept a third of the stars from the sky, tossing them to the earth. And the dragon stood before the woman who was about to give birth, ready to devour her child as soon as she gave birth."
-Revelation 12:3-4 BSB

Satan deceived one third of the angels in heaven to follow him. Those are the ones that are identified in the Scriptures as demons. The word demons means evil spirits, who are fallen angels, as seen in **Revelation 12:7**, in which a big war takes place in heaven in the end times. Satan attempts to take over God's throne but loses that war. The dragon (who is Satan), with his fallen angels, fights against Michael and his angels. The word demon, as seen above, shows the state [character] of Satan's fallen angels. After the angels abandoned God, most likely before the creation of Adam, they became pure evil with hatred towards God and his followers in heaven and on earth.

"And the angels who did not stay within their own domain but abandoned their proper dwelling—these He has kept in eternal chains under darkness, bound for judgment on that great day."
-Jude 1:6 BSB

Some angels got judged immediately—like those mentioned in the **Book of Jude** and the **Book of 2 Peter**—for corrupting humanity in the days of Noah when they abandoned their positions in heaven.

"4 For if God did not spare the angels when they sinned, but cast them deep into hell, placing them in chains of darkness to be held for judgment; 5 if He did not spare the ancient world when He brought the flood on its ungodly people, but preserved Noah, a preacher of righteousness, among the eight" **-2 Peter 2:4-5 BSB**

When we go to Genesis 6, it reveals why the angels rebelled against the LORD.

"Now when men began to multiply on the face of the earth and daughters were born to them, 2 <u>**the sons of God saw that the daughters of men were beautiful, and they took as wives whomever they chose**</u>. 3 So the LORD said, "My Spirit will not contend with man forever, for he is mortal; his days shall be 120 years." 4 The Nephilim were on the earth in those days—and afterward as well—when the sons of God had relations with the daughters of men. And they bore them children who became the mighty men of old, men of renown." **-Genesis 6:1-4 BSB**

In verse 2, the phrase "the sons of God" refers to angels as seen in the **Book of Job 1:6**, which says, "6 One day the sons of God came to present themselves before the LORD, and Satan also came with them."

28.

The phrase "they took as wives whomever they chose" could be explained in a couple of ways. First of all, we see that angels were not created to procreate. We see this in **Matthew 22:30**, which says, "30 In the resurrection, people will neither marry nor be given in marriage. Instead, they will be like the angels in heaven."

So how can angels (fallen angels) in **Genesis 6** take wives for themselves? Either they possessed human bodies or transformed their bodies so that they were able to have relations with their wives, and their children were the men of renown or famous ones.

The phrase "The Nephilim" means the giants (who are not the results of angels having relations with the daughters of men). The construction of **verse 4** cannot suggest that the Nephilim are the angel's offspring because it says, "The Nephilim were on the earth in those days—and afterward as well—when the sons of God had relations with the daughters of men. And they bore them children who became the mighty men of old, men of renown."

It says that the Nephilim were already there when the sons of God (the fallen angels) took wives for themselves and had famous children. The Nephilim, whomever they were, continued to exist until the flood came upon the earth, which wiped out humanity (except for Noah and his family) and put the sons of God, the fallen angels, in chains in hell (**2 Peter 2:4-5**).

In **Numbers 13:32-33**, it says, "32 So they gave the Israelites a bad report about the land that they had spied out: "The land we explored devours its inhabitants, and all the people we saw there are great in stature. 33 We even saw the Nephilim there—the descendants of Anak that come from the Nephilim! We seemed like grasshoppers in our own sight, and we must have seemed the same to them!"

We must understand that everyone in the post-flood era was judged and destroyed, and the sons of God (fallen angels) were cast into hell and chained up until judgment day. So, the word "Nephilim" mentioned in **Numbers 13:33** suggests that the people there were giants, and it reminded the Israelites of the portion of Scripture that spoke about the Nephilim. The Bible records that only eight people survived the flood.

Genesis 6 gives us a picture of how angels became bad and how they were judged in the time of the flood for making men evil through their influence of sexual immorality.

Lust for a believer in Christ comes through images that are placed in their minds by demons. These creatures fell because they also lusted after women to experience that which was forbidden to them (Genesis 6:2). When a person lusts, they are carrying out the desire implanted by demonic influence.

Not all of the fallen angels participated in the time of the Nephilim. There seem to have been two rebellions in heaven. The first happened when Satan deceived them and was kicked out of heaven. The second wave was when they got tempted by the daughters of men and abandoned God for them. The demons of today are the angels of the first wave of the rebellion who deceives the world through idolatry (the worship of idols), false religion, and the desires of the flesh.

"While Israel was staying in Shittim, the men began to indulge in sexual immorality with the daughters of Moab, 2 who also invited them to the sacrifices for their gods. And the people ate and bowed down to these gods. 3 So Israel joined in worshiping Baal of Peor, and the anger of the LORD burned against them." **-Numbers 25:1-3 BSB**

Demonic worship has two components. The first one is aimed at one's sexual lust, and the second is through the worship of idols, self, or materialism. The demons use sex to entice an individual to stray completely from the Lord. Their main goal through lust is to get you to worship something else, like your fleshy desires, rather than Jesus Christ, the one true God.

Demons dwell behind every idol to take away the worship due to God towards them through idolatry which the demons have put in men's hearts to create.

"They sacrificed to demons, not to God, to gods they had not known, to newly arrived gods, which your fathers did not fear."
-Deuteronomy 32:17 BSB

Foreign gods are idols.

"19 Am I suggesting, then, that food sacrificed to an idol is anything, or that an idol is anything? 20 No, but the sacrifices of pagans are offered to demons, not to God. And I do not want you to be participants with demons." **-1 Corinthians 10:19-20 BSB**

The demons, by Satan's command, have just one purpose. It is to make you abandon the Lord Jesus Christ and His Word so you will be unable to do His will (Genesis 3). They want you to rebel just as they did because of their hatred toward God.

Part 2: Demons And The Tactics They Use To Entrap You

33.

"The tempter came to Him and said, "If You are the Son of God, tell these stones to become bread." -**Matthew 4:3 BSB**

Demons will not come to you until they see an opportunity. This opportunity happens when you stop reading the Scriptures and skip many days of prayer. They will continue observing you, and when they see your faith dip to a certain degree, that's when they attack you.

One of their attacks is to question your status with God. Satan asked Jesus to prove that He was the Son of God. The devil already knows who He is, but He wanted Jesus to do a miracle instead of relying on the Father to provide for Him. Demons will try to get you to depend on yourself and not wait on the Lord. If you do that, it will show a lack of faith on your part.

"But Jesus answered, "It is written: 'Man shall not live on bread alone, but on every word that comes from the mouth of God.'" -**Matthew 4:4 BSB**

When Satan set his trap for Jesus, the Son of God answered back with Scripture. God's Word is the only weapon we have that will give us the truth so we won't get deceived. God's Word keeps us from falling into his traps by lighting up our path to see all of the enemy's pitfalls.

"5 Then the devil took Him to the holy city and set Him on the pinnacle of the temple. 6 "If You are the Son of God," he said, "throw Yourself down. For it is written: 'He will command His angels concerning You, and they will lift You up in their hands, so that You will not strike Your foot against a stone.'" -**Matthew 4:5-6 BSB**

The devil will test your faith to see if he can deceive you by twisting Scripture to say something other than what it means. That's how he uses the false teachers. They will quote the Bible but interpret it in a way that will fit their agenda. They use the Word of God for gain—to take something from you that they want. Jesus defeated Satan's attack by going back to God's Word (verse 7) to show him how he had distorted it.

The end goal for the devil is to get you to worship him instead of the Lord Jesus Christ. Just like Satan betrayed the Lord, so he wants you to betray Him as well. The devil wants you to be evil and dark. He hates the light and anything good. The devil wants to destroy you because he knows that the Lake of Fire is awaiting him, and he doesn't want to be the only one there. He wants you to join him.

35.

WHAT IS DEMONIC OPPRESSION?

Demonic Oppression

Oppression is not the same as possession. Why? Possession signifies that you are no longer in control of your behavior and movements of your body.

Possession

"17 Someone in the crowd replied, "Teacher, I brought You my son, who has a spirit that makes him mute. 18 Whenever it seizes him, it throws him to the ground. He foams at the mouth, gnashes his teeth, and becomes rigid. I asked Your disciples to drive it out, but they were unable."...22 "It often throws him into the fire or into the water, trying to kill him. But if You can do anything, have compassion on us and help us." -**Mark 9:17-18, 22 BSB**

Oppression means being assaulted heavily with extreme **physical**, **mental**, **financial**, and **emotional** problems with no sense of hope. Those are the devices that demons use to destroy your faith in Christ Jesus and render you as a Christian spiritually useless for the kingdom of God.

Below are a few examples of demonic oppression, then I will go into more detail.

"After the Spirit of the LORD had departed from Saul, a spirit of distress from the LORD began to **torment** him." **-1 Samuel 16:14 BSB**

The Hebrew word for torment is **Baath** which means **to fall upon, startle, terrify**. *Strongs# 1204*

In King Saul's case, he was being tormented by fear.

"Or because of these surpassingly great revelations. So to keep me from becoming conceited, I was given a **thorn** in my flesh, a messenger of Satan, to **torment** me." **-2 Corinthians 12:7 BSB**

The word **thorn** in Greek gives the meaning of being afflicted physically, which connects with the word torment, as found in the same verse. The Greek word **torment** means **to strike with a fist**. Paul's demonic oppression was employing physical pain.

King Saul was being tormented mentally, going mad, and Paul was being tormented physically so we see that oppression can be both in the mind and the body.

There was a person who was oppressed by Satan himself. Satan oppressed Job with ALL of the categories mentioned at the beginning of this chapter. Job was hit head on with all of Satan's storms of destruction. The devil had full intent to completely wipe out his faith in God.

38.

Let's take a closer look at Job's demonic oppression, which will reveal Satan's tactics.

"8 Then the LORD said to Satan, "Have you considered My servant Job? For there is no one on earth like him, a man who is blameless and upright, who fears God and shuns evil." 9 Satan answered the LORD, "Does Job fear God for nothing? 10 Have You not placed a hedge on every side around him and his household and all that he owns? You have blessed the work of his hands, and his possessions have increased in the land. 11 But stretch out Your hand and strike all that he has, and he will surely curse You to Your face." 12 "Very well," said the LORD to Satan. "Everything he has is in your hands, but you must not lay a hand on the man himself." Then Satan went out from the presence of the LORD." **-Job 1:8-12 BSB**

Financially Oppressed–**Job 1:14-17**, "14 a messenger came and reported to Job: "While the oxen were plowing and the donkeys were grazing nearby, 15 the Sabeans swooped down and took them away. They put the servants to the sword, and I alone have escaped to tell you!" 16 While he was still speaking, another messenger came and reported: "The fire of God fell from heaven. It burned and consumed the sheep and the servants, and I alone have escaped to tell you!" 17 While he was still speaking, another messenger came and reported: "The Chaldeans formed three bands, raided the camels, and took them away. They put the servants to the sword, and I alone have escaped to tell you!"

Emotionally Oppressed–Job 1:18-19, "18 While he was still speaking, another messenger came and reported: "Your sons and daughters were eating and drinking wine in their oldest brother's house, 19 when suddenly a mighty wind swept in from the desert and struck the four corners of the house. It collapsed on the young people and they are dead, and I alone have escaped to tell you!"

Mentally Oppressed–Job 4:13-14, "13 In disquieting visions in the night, when deep sleep falls on men, 14 fear and trembling came over me and made all my bones shudder."

Physically Oppressed–Job 2:6-8, 6 "Very well," said the LORD to Satan. "He is in your hands, but you must spare his life." 7 So Satan went out from the presence of the LORD and infected Job with terrible boils from the soles of his feet to the crown of his head. 8 And Job took a piece of broken pottery to scrape himself as he sat among the ashes."

Every Christian will get oppressed by demons for the sole purpose of destroying their faith. When you feel a heavy burden of fear and worry, know that you are being demonically oppressed.

Not all sicknesses or any other type of bodily pain suggest that you are being demonically oppressed. Only when that pain of any kind results in doubting God's love towards you. That would constitute being demonically oppressed. Demons may not cause the illness or physical pain, but they will take advantage of it and try to make you abandon God.

40.

Christians should never worry about losing their faith because Jesus promised that the same way He overcame the world, so shall we, for His Spirit lives inside us.

"I have told you these things so that in Me you may have peace. In the world you will have tribulation. But take courage; I have overcome the world!" **-John 16:33 BSB**

"I am writing to you, fathers, because you know Him who is from the beginning. I am writing to you, young men, because you have overcome the evil one. I have written to you, children, because you know the Father." **-1 John 2:13 BSB**

41.

Can A Christian Be possessed By A Demon?

42.

"Meanwhile, Moses was shepherding the flock of his father-in-law Jethro, the priest of Midian. He led the flock to the far side of the wilderness and came to Horeb, the mountain of God. 2 There the angel of the LORD appeared to him in a blazing fire from within a bush. Moses saw the bush ablaze with fire, but it was not consumed. 3 So Moses thought, "I must go over and see this marvelous sight. Why is the bush not burning up?" 4 When the LORD saw that he had gone over to look, God called out to him from within the bush, "Moses, Moses!" "Here I am," he answered. 5 "Do not come any closer," God said. "Take off your sandals, for the place where you are standing is holy ground." **-Exodus 3:1-5 BSB**

When God touched the ground, there was a radius around the bush that became holy and was separated from the rest of the ground. Anything that God touches becomes like Him, holy. When Moses saw the burning bush and heard the voice of God calling him and went toward God's direction, he was warned by God not to step on the ground that was made holy by God's presence. Moses was instructed to take off his sandals which carried dirt that wasn't made holy and was prohibited from mixing in the dirt under his sandals with the rest that was under God.

Insight: Holy

Holy means to be set apart for God's use, and it also refers to being made clean by having our sins forgiven in Christ Jesus. God must clean us up first before we can become effective.

43.

When the Holy Spirit dwells in a believer, the inner man is made holy because of the presence of God. That is seen in **1 Corinthians 3:16-17**, which says, "16 Do you not know that you yourselves are God's temple, and that God's Spirit dwells in you? 17 If anyone destroys God's temple, God will destroy him; for God's temple is holy, and you are that temple."

Anything unauthorized or unclean (*evil spirits/demons*) cannot take residence within us, where we have been made holy due to the Holy Spirit's presence in our hearts.

44.

Demons Are Like Ninjas

45.

"If you do what is right, will you not be accepted? But if you refuse to do what is right, sin is crouching at your door; it desires you, but you must master it." **-Genesis 4:7 BSB**

This passage describes sin with animalistic characteristics to paint a picture of a demon desiring to destroy the relationship of two brothers, Cain and Abel. For Satan to have access to Cain, he had to get real close and wait until the right moment to strike. His relationship with the Lord wasn't right so God wouldn't accept his sacrifice. Satan took advantage of that. Satan used Cain's uncontrolled anger to murder his brother Abel because God accepted Abel's gift (sacrifice) over Cain's, which made him depressed and turned into anger.

Satan will take any opportunity with stealth to attack your faith.

Demons are just like ninjas. They spy on the believers in Jesus Christ and gather intel on the best way to advance in their attacks. They also evaluate the Christians' lives for weaknesses [gaps] in their faith for an entryway.

46.

What are ninjas? They were warriors who were hired to fight unconventional warfare.

These were their roles.

Espionage: The Ninjas would spy on their enemies for gaps or weaknesses in the walls to gather information on the terrain.

Deception: They would disguise themselves to look like their enemies to enter their castle and evaluate the situation to set it on fire for its destruction.

Surprise attacks: The ninjas would operate in the darkness for cloaking purposes to get close to their enemies and capture them or kill them.

The demons will send you a false Christian to access your personal life and carry out deception. A false Christian will introduce a false Jesus to make you follow that Jesus over the one revealed in the Scriptures.

"4 For if someone comes and proclaims a Jesus other than the One we proclaimed, or if you receive a different spirit than the One you received, or a different gospel than the one you accepted, you put up with it way too easily." **-2 Corinthins 11:4 BSB**

After the demons have gathered all of the information needed on you, they will commence the spiritual attack for the destruction of your faith in Christ. These demons are very deadly. You won't see the attack coming, only when it already occurred, making it too late. Unless you are in prayer, reading the Scriptures daily, their attacks will get you by surprise.

47.

WHY SATAN WANTS YOU TO DOUBT THE BIBLE

48.

"Now the serpent was more crafty than any beast of the field that the LORD God had made. And he said to the woman, "**Did God really say**, 'You must not eat from any tree in the garden?'"
-Genesis 3:1 BSB

Satan attacked Eve by planting doubt in her mind about what God said. He continued with his attack by giving her the wrong interpretation to bring doubt and confusion to deteriorate Eve's trust in God's Word, as seen in **Genesis 3:4**, which says, "You will not surely die," the serpent told her."

If we start to doubt God's Word, we won't be protected from deception because trusting in the Word of God equips us with the Full Armor of God (**Ephesians 6:10-18**), which shields us from being hit by the arrows of lies that constantly bombard us to kill our faith and trust in the Scriptures.

Once our protection (Armor of God) is off, Satan then introduces us to doctrines of demons seen in **1 Timothy 4:1**, "Now the Spirit expressly states that in later times some will abandon the faith to follow deceitful spirits and the teachings of demons."

When Eve's protection was removed by doubt, she was no longer capable of distinguishing between a correct and false interpretation of the Word of God. She ate the fruit from the Tree of the Knowledge of Good and Evil that God forbade her to eat. The danger of not believing in the Inerrancy of Scripture is so grave that you will lose your basis to weigh sound doctrine from false doctrine since you won't measure any spiritual message with your rod or ruler—that is the Scriptures—because you no longer have trust in it.

49.

The word **Canon** (The Bible) in Greek it's called **kanón**, which means (lit: a level, ruler), a rule, regulation, rule of conduct or doctrine, (b) a measured (defined) area, province. *Strong's #2583*

Why would a carpenter use a ruler that he feels is inaccurate? Satan attacks the credibility of the Bible to keep you from measuring his lies, therefore, blindsiding you from seeing the trap set before you with the ultimate goal of spiritually destroying you by giving you a [spiritual] poisoned fruit to eat.

We must stand firm on the Word of God without doubting it like Jesus when He was being tempted by Satan in the wilderness. We see this in **Matthew 4:3-4**, which says, "3 The tempter came to Him and said, "If You are the Son of God, tell these stones to become bread." 4 But Jesus answered, "It is written: 'Man shall not live on bread alone, but on every word that comes from the mouth of God.'"

By Jesus turning the stone into bread, He would have sinned against God because His reliance would have been on His abilities rather than on God's promises. Jesus, in turn, fought back by quoting scripture because He trusted in them, and so should we.

Satan struck again by quoting **Psalms 91:11-12** and giving the wrong interpretation to attempt to deceive Jesus into sin. Jesus once again quoted scripture to correct Satan's false interpretation. Christians must know the Bible like Jesus, but how can we ever learn it if we doubt its inerrancy in the first place? Jesus quoted it because He trusted its accuracy.

50.

When a person rejects the inerrant Word of God by doubting it, Satan will immediately introduce heresy to snatch whatever truth there is in them. Since the person doesn't trust the Bible to protect him by putting on the Full Armor of God, he will eat up the fruit of Satan's heresy, and spiritual death is inevitable, destroying his family in the process. When the head of the family (the husband) falls, the rest of his household follows.

"7 If you remain in Me and My words remain in you, ask whatever you wish, and it will be done for you. 8 This is to My Father's glory, that you bear much fruit, proving yourselves to be My disciples." **-John 15:7-8 BSB**

If anyone claims to be a follower of Jesus but denies the inerrancy of scripture, I would seriously doubt their salvation. The only one who has a pure hatred for God's Word is Satan. He will go to any length to discredit and make you doubt it.

51.

The Demon Of Flattery

52.

Demons will take their names from the special attacks they are known by—the temptations they use against the believers. For an example of this, let us look at **Mark 9.**

"When Jesus saw that a crowd had come running, He rebuked the unclean spirit. "You deaf and mute spirit," He said, "I command you to come out and never enter him again." **-Mark 9:25 BSB**

As you can see in **Mark 9:25**, Jesus encounters a demon called deaf and mute because that was his specialty in attacking people.

The arsenal the demon decides to employ toward a believer in Jesus Christ will make him aware of what type of demon he is facing, helping him confront it properly.

There are demons called flattery who are very deadly to a believer's faith because they will come to you with praises, insincere ones, to make you prideful and rob God of His glory. They want you to accept your gifts as if you manufactured them yourself instead of acknowledging that it was given to you by the Lord.

"For such people are not serving our Lord Christ, but their own appetites. By smooth talk and flattery they deceive the hearts of the naive." **-Romans 16:18 BSB**

The word *flattery* in **Romans 16** is used as a tactic for deception by dividing people (verse 17) from genuine believers to come to their side and eventually believe in their false doctrines.

53.

"A man who flatters his neighbor spreads a net for his feet."
-Proverbs 29:5 BSB

Flattery is a trap set to capture you so that you will become disabled and won't be able to carry out God's plan for your life. But, for an individual who is close to salvation, it can turn out extremely bad, like the elimination of having faith in Jesus Christ to keep the person from receiving eternal life and staying in an unregenerated state until death.

The only way to combat the demon of flattery is to keep in mind that the person you have become and everything you possess has been given to you from above. Always give glory to the Lord Jesus Christ for everything. That mindset will keep you from stumbling.

54.

Satan's Lie: You Can Become Like God

You Must Believe That Jesus Is God Or You Cannot Be Saved

The New Age religion collects other teachings from different religions that would agree with their philosophy and the way they think about God. They adopt a false God and Jesus from false religions. That is the major problem they have, because if you get Jesus Christ wrong, you will die in your sins.

Let's look at what Jesus said in **John 8:24**, "That is why I told you that you would die in your sins. For unless you believe that I am He, you will die in your sins."

Who did Jesus claim to be? In **John 14:8**, Philip asked Jesus to show them the Father, referring to God. Jesus responded to Philip that he has already seen God. This is what Jesus said to Philip in verse 9, "Jesus replied, "Philip, I have been with you all this time, and still you do not know Me? Anyone who has seen Me has seen the Father. How can you say, 'Show us the Father'?

Jesus told Philip that he had already seen God [the Father]. Jesus told him that seeing Him is seeing God, so how can he [Philip] ask Him to see God? For he had already witnessed Him in Jesus Christ.

If you do not believe that Jesus is God, you cannot get saved because you will believe in another Jesus that doesn't exist.

New Age Teaches That You Are God

In one of their New Age teachings, they say that we are all God. That is not only unbiblical but demonic. This is not new from Satan because it goes back to Genesis Chapter 3 when the serpent went to Eve to deceive her by telling her that she can become like God.

"For God knows that in the day you eat of it, your eyes will be opened and you will be like God, knowing good and evil."
-Genesis 3:5 BSB

The New Age religion has elements of occultism in beliefs and practices

That concept that you can be like God, having Godlike wisdom, comes from Satan himself and is a BIG lie which will send you to hell.

We were created in God's image (**Genesis 1:27**), but that does not mean that we have the Godlike qualities that make Him who He is. For He is All-Knowing, All-Powerful, and God is everywhere at the same time (not that He is everything, but is everywhere). God was never created. He always existed, and through Him, all things came into existence.

57.

"In the beginning was the Word, and the Word was with God, and the Word was God. 2 He was with God in the beginning. 3 Through Him all things were made, and without Him nothing was made that has been made...14 The Word became flesh and made His dwelling among us. We have seen His glory, the glory of the one and only Sonc from the Father, full of grace and truth." -**John 1:1-3, 14 BSB**

Satan Blinds The unbeliever So That They Cannot Get Saved

Another religion that teaches you can become a god is Mormonism. These religions are directed by demons to deceive everyone they can. They want to blind the people so that they won't accept the truth of the gospel when it is preached to them so that they will be convinced that the lie is the truth. So to them, the lie is the truth, and the truth is the lie, and up is down, and down is up. The scariest thing is to believe you are in the truth, but after death you will realize that you were wrong when it's too late.

"The god of this age has blinded the minds of unbelievers so they cannot see the light of the gospel of the glory of Christ, who is the image of God." -**2 Corinthians 4:4 BSB**

Salvation Is Found Only In Jesus Christ

The reason why the forces of evil want to deceive us is that they want us to be damned like they are.

58.

We are not, nor can we become God. We are humans, and that's it. We have a spirit that will live forever, either with Jesus Christ in heaven or apart from Him in hell. It is your choice. Don't believe in the lie. Believe in what the Scripture says.

"Jesus answered, "I am the way and the truth and the life. No one comes to the Father except through Me." **-John 14:6 BSB**

If we were gods, we wouldn't need Jesus to save us, would we? But, since we are not God and cannot become like God, we need to trust in Jesus Christ. Only He can give us eternal life.

59.

Satan Is Like A Shark

"8 Be sober-minded and alert. Your adversary the devil prowls around like a roaring lion, seeking someone to devour. 9 Resist him, standing firm in your faith and in the knowledge that your brothers throughout the world are undergoing the same kinds of suffering." **-1 Peter 5:8-9 BSB**

Sharks are always on the lookout for any sign of blood—smelling it from miles and miles away, which will take the shark to its victim. In **Job 1:6-7**, God asked Satan his whereabouts on the earth, and Satan replied, ."7...From roaming through the earth," he replied, "and walking back and forth in it."

Just like a shark, he travels looking for a victim to devour. Satan wants to kill people—for a Christian, he wants to kill his faith in Christ, and for an unbeliever to make sure he doesn't believe in Jesus Christ and get saved.

The unbeliever has no chance to fight against the devil unless he surrenders his life to Jesus. But for a believer, the devil has to think twice about his attacks against him. Christians have weapons to fight off the devil, and those weapons are The Full Armor of God. With it, we can protect ourselves and strike back.

Imagine a boat out at sea, and a great white shark starts ramming itself into that boat. The people in the boat will be very scared because they know the moment they fall into the water, they are dead meat. Now, imagine a different boat this time, equipped with harpoons.

61.

Not only does the boat carry harpoons, but each person on board has a long stick with a sharp end that carries electricity to stab the shark when it gets too close. Any shark that comes against that boat armed with weapons won't last too long. I guarantee you, the shark will either be killed or will flee.

The devil will cause pain in our lives. We have to realize that we are not the only ones going through tribulation. Many other believers are under attack by the enemy. Jesus commands us to persevere, trusting in the Lord to carry us through it. Never give in to despair.

THE TRUE VIRUS "THE DEVIL"

"You belong to your father, the devil, and you want to carry out his desires. He was a murderer from the beginning, refusing to uphold the truth, because there is no truth in him. When he lies, he speaks his native language, because he is a liar and the father of lies."
-John 8:44 BSB

The serpent, the devil who is Satan, murdered Adam and Eve in the very beginning by making them stumble through deception. He killed their relationship with God. Sin invaded their lives and induced spiritual and physical death.

4 "Skin for skin!" Satan replied. "A man will give up all he owns in exchange for his life. 5 But stretch out Your hand and strike his flesh and bones, and he will surely curse You to Your face." 6 "Very well," said the LORD to Satan. "He is in your hands, but you must spare his life." 7 So Satan went out from the presence of the LORD and infected Job with terrible boils from the soles of his feet to the crown of his head." **-Job 2:4-7 BSB**

The Virus

Satan attacks men's health to cause suffering so that the blame may be focused back on God to denounce one's faith in Him. This attack is designed specifically for believers in Christ Jesus.

God's Purpose

God allows such attacks for the Christian's growth. Without it, our faith cannot be pushed, compelling us to trust in Jesus, which develops and builds us up into a mature men in Christ.

The Lord Jesus Christ is in control. Prayer has to be the center of our life and devotion to the LORD. God's Word must be our anchor so that we won't drift away from sound doctrine (teachings) and find ourselves in a deceived state, which would make our situation that much worse.

TAKE HEART, JESUS CHRIST WILL NEVER LEAVE YOU

The Virus, the devil, is always looking for a way to destroy us, to make us ineffective for the kingdom of God.

"Be sober-minded and alert. Your adversary the devil prowls around like a roaring lion, seeking someone to devour." **-1 Peter 5:8 BSB**

65.

How Well Are You Protected From Deception?

"Now there were also false prophets among the people, just as there will be false teachers among you. They will secretly introduce destructive heresies, even denying the Master who bought them—bringing swift destruction on themselves." **-2 Peter 2:1 BSB**

If you have a computer, you will need to install an antivirus to catch viruses before they corrupt your computer and make it unusable. We are like a computer, having a system that is designed by God to function correctly for His use. Satan is like a hacker who tries to inject his viruses to interrupt your ability, as a Christian, to do God's will which is bringing others to Christ.

"Beloved, do not believe every spirit, but test the spirits to see whether they are from God. For many false prophets have gone out into the world." **-1 John 4:1 BSB**

Your antivirus has to be updated daily to be prepared to defend your computer from all types of killer viruses. As believers, the way we update our minds to defeat false doctrine—viruses—is by reading the Scriptures every day. It will put your mind at its optimal level with knowing the Scriptures—being well versed to combat deception which twists the Scriptures.

"I am afraid, however, that just as Eve was deceived by the serpent's cunning, your minds may be led astray from your simple and pure devotion to Christ." **-2 Corinthians 11:3 BSB**

67.

The purpose of the disruption of the virus that the devil injects is to disconnect your WiFi. Your WiFi represents your connection with the Lord through prayer. If deception takes place, your prayer life will be affected. You won't be able to connect with the Lord as you will be praying to the wrong Jesus.

"20 O Timothy, guard what has been entrusted to you. Avoid irreverent, empty chatter and the opposing arguments of so-called "knowledge," 21 which some have professed and thus swerved away from the faith. Grace be with you all." **-1 Timothy 6:20-21 BSB**

What's coming to the earth will be something that we have never experienced before, testing our faith to its limit. Update daily your knowledge of God's Word, which feeds your faith. Keep praying for direction and protection, spreading the gospel to save as many as possible before the rapture comes. Everything that is happening in the world is pointing to the one who is prophesied to come in the End-Times, the Antichrist.

68.

SATAN'S THREE STEPS TO DECEPTION

69.

"Now the Spirit expressly states that in later times some will abandon the faith to follow deceitful spirits and the teachings of demons, 2 influenced by the hypocrisy of liars, whose consciences are seared with a hot iron. 3 They will prohibit marriage and require abstinence from certain foods that God has created to be received with thanksgiving by those who believe and know the truth." **-1 Timothy 4:1-3 BSB**

There's a three-step process that demons take in the hopes of killing one's faith for good. The false teachers they use have to deconstruct the truth from your mind and replace it with theirs, or else it won't work. We will look at **1 Timothy 4**, verses 1 through 3, to show the enemy's three-step to deception.

Step Number 1 (*teachings of demons*): Satan and his demons will come up with a false doctrine that closely resembles God's Word so that it would be more palatable for Christians and non-Christians as if it's a message from God.

Step Number 2 (*hypocrisy of liars*): To get their deceptive message out to people, they will handpick a pseudo-Christian, a false prophet, or teacher, who is easily deceived. They are the ones who continue to be in bondage (i.e., morally defeated by the desires of the flesh). Some of the sins that these pseudo-Christians are shackled to are as follows: the love of money, sexual immorality, being famous (which is to be loved by the world and to be praised by men), and many other things like it.

These false prophets have no problem having one foot in the Lord and the other in the world to satisfy their sinful cravings.

"21 Not everyone who says to Me, 'Lord, Lord,' will enter the kingdom of heaven, but only he who does the will of My Father in heaven. 22 Many will say to Me on that day, 'Lord, Lord, did we not prophesy in Your name, and in Your name drive out demons and perform many miracles?' 23 Then I will tell them plainly, 'I never knew you; depart from Me, you workers of lawlessness!' "
-**Matthew 7:21-23 BSB**

Step Number 3 (*They will prohibit marriage and require abstinence from certain foods*): Their false teachings entail an outward appearance of "righteousness" that will make them seem godly to others.

It promotes abstinence from marriage to some clergymen or for others, and to abstain from certain foods as a way for the demons to make them feel closer to God, but in reality, they are falling deeper into deceit. They will make you think that holiness comes from changing one's outside appearance instead of the inside to reflect God's morals.

There are many false teachers out there, and if you are a Christian, you are a big target. You must take strong measures to protect yourself by seeking the Lord, knowing His Word, and staying in prayer. The closer you get to Jesus, the safer you will be.

The End Times

Which Death Do You Prefer?

"13 And the second beast performed great signs to cause even fire from heaven to come down to earth in the presence of the people. 14 Because of the signs it was given to perform on behalf of the first beast, it deceived those who dwell on the earth, telling them to make an image to the beast that had been wounded by the sword and yet had lived. 15 The second beast was permitted to give breath to the image of the first beast, so that the image could speak and cause all who refused to worship it to be killed." **-Revelation 13:13-15 BSB**

The Antichrist's false prophet will perform great miracles and wonders to awe the people to get them to give their allegiance to the Antichrist. After an idol is made in the likeness of the Antichrist, a demon will enter that idol and make it speak with authority.

It will give everybody the option to either receive the mark of the beast (which would permanently reserve a place in hell for them), or choose to reject the mark of the beast because of Jesus and pay for it with their lives (which will have them end up in heaven).

In the Great Tribulation, one's decision for Jesus will make all the difference between life and death. Both decisions contain death, but only one will result in eternal life. If you choose to get the 666, you will forever be separated from the presence of God—spiritually dead in the flames of fire (**Revelation 14:9-12**). But if you decide to die for Jesus Christ by rejecting the beast's mark, you will gain eternal life after your death.

Which death do you prefer?

THE END TIMES

What Does The Number 666 mean?

"Here is a call for wisdom: Let the one who has insight calculate the number of the beast, for it is the number of a man, and that number is 666." **-Revelation 13:18 BSB**

Why did the beast, the Antichrist, choose not only the number 6 but the number three times?

We will look very closely at two specific words and the three numbers—the beast, man, and 666.

The number 6 in creation is when God created the beasts of the earth and man.

[**The Six Day Of Creation**] "24 And God said, "Let the earth bring forth living creatures according to their kinds: livestock, land crawlers, and **beasts** of the earth according to their kinds." And it was so. 25 God made the **beasts** of the earth according to their kinds, the livestock according to their kinds, and everything that crawls upon the earth according to its kind. And God saw that it was good. 26 Then God said, "Let Us make **man** in Our image, after Our likeness, to rule over the fish of the sea and the birds of the air, over the livestock, and over all the earth itself and every creature that crawls upon it." **-Genesis 1:24-26 BSB**

The Seventh Day Of Creation

"And by the seventh day God had finished the work He had been doing; so on that day He rested from all His work." **-Genesis 2:2 BSB**

The number 7 (the seventh day) in creation is when God finished creating everything and rested, so the word "rested" here means to cease.

Satan chose the number 6 to represent himself, the Antichrist, and the false prophet as it is short of the number 7, which represents God. The number 6 is man-centered.

The Greek number 666 is written as 600 (Strong's #1812), 60 (Strong's #1835), 6 (Strong's #1803). The Greek has it as 600, 60, 6 (666).

The reason why there are three numbers—600, 60, and 6—is that there are three enemies: the Dragon (Satan), the Antichrist (the first beast), and the false prophet (the second beast). The highest number is 600, which represents the Dragon.

The number 60 represents the Antichrist because he will rule for Satan, and the number 6 represents the false prophet because he will promote the Antichrist. Since Satan is the one who gives the first and second beast their power and authority, he corresponds to the number 600, as their power comes from him.

Also, if you look at **Genesis 3:1-6**, the serpent (Satan) wanted Eve and her husband Adam to take what he was offering to kill them spiritually.

In Revelation, Satan will impose a mandate on the human race to receive something that will kill them spiritually. In Genesis it was the forbidden fruit, and in Revelation it's the mark of the beast that will send people to hell for all eternity if taken.

In conclusion, the number 666 represents a world without God and Satan as its ruler. Satan's plan since the creation was to plunge mankind into darkness so that humanity as a whole would end up in hell for all eternity.

THE END TIMES

THE END TIMES APOSTASY

"Let no one deceive you in any way, for it will not come until the rebellion occurs and the man of lawlessness—the son of destruction—is revealed." **-2 Thessalonians 2:3 BSB**

The rapture (**1 Thessalonians 4:16-18 & 2 Thessalonians 2:1**) is the event when Jesus will take the Christians to heaven to be with Him forever before the seven-year Tribulation.

The phrase "for it will not come" refers to the Great Tribulation, which will not occur "until the rebellion" (or apostasy) takes place, and right after that, the Antichrist appears on the world stage to sign a seven-year treaty with Israel and the surrounding nations for "peace" (a false peace). Before those things happen, the rapture will take place (**1 Thessalonians 1:10**).

The homosexual agenda belongs to Satan, and he has brought it to the churches to make the hearts of those who are not anchored in Christ turn away from Him. The devil will take many professing Christians to hell by convincing them that sexual immorality is not sinful, thus deceiving them to accept that which the Word of God has condemned.

Right before Jesus comes, there will be fewer Christians on earth (**Luke 18:8**) who will be the ones to get raptured. Satan wants many people to go to hell with him, and the sad part about it is that he will be successful.

"I tell you, He will promptly carry out justice on their behalf. Nevertheless, when the Son of Man comes, will He find faith on earth?" **-Luke 18:8 BSB**

79.

Imagine you go to the kitchen and you see a basket full of apples. You think that you have many apples, but as you look more into the basket, you notice that the ones at the bottom are all rotten. The apples at the top are good, but the ones at the bottom are bad. Only a few apples are good to eat. That is what's happening to Christianity. Many people claim to be Christians, but as **2 Thessalonians 2** says, many will apostatize, showing that only a few are genuinely saved.

If you call yourself a Christian, you better understand that the devil has targeted you to destroy your faith by having you accept another "truth" that opposes what the Scripture teaches.

How grounded are you in Christ? You better start digging yourself real firm and deep in the Word of God because the enemy will try his hardest you pull you out of it.

THE END TIMES

A Worldwide Collapse Will Introduce The Mark Of The Beast

"16 And the second beast required all people small and great, rich and poor, free and slave, to receive a mark on their right hand or on their forehead, 17 so that no one could buy or sell unless he had the mark—the name of the beast or the number of its name. 18 Here is a call for wisdom: Let the one who has insight calculate the number of the beast, for it is the number of a man, and that number is 666." **-Revelation 13:16-18 BSB**

The Mark of the Beast will be connected to a currency for buying and selling that will be new to the world as it will be put in the human body—the right hand or the forehead. For that to happen, there must be a worldwide economic collapse.

Satan always uses worldly riches to get people to worship him. He tried that with Jesus in the Book of **Matthew 4:8-9**, where he offered Jesus riches for worship. Jesus replied, "Away from Me, Satan!" Jesus declared. "For it is written: 'Worship the Lord your God and serve Him only.' " **-Matthew 4:10 BSB**

Undoubtedly, he will do it again, and it will be for the whole world but will come with a clause. The clause will be that if you do not worship the Antichrist through the system that he will set in place (like worshiping his image and receiving his mark on your body), you will pay for it with your life. See **Revelation 13:7-10.**

82.

If you reject the Mark of the Beast, his name, or his number (666), you won't be able to work and eat. Are you willing to starve than to take it? Is food much more important to you than going to heaven? **Revelation 14:9-12** states that if you receive the Antichrist mark on your body, you will forfeit your chance to go to heaven permanently.

"9 And a third angel followed them, calling out in a loud voice, "If anyone worships the beast and its image, and receives its mark on his forehead or on his hand, 10 he too will drink the wine of God's anger, poured undiluted into the cup of His wrath. And he will be tormented in fire and sulfur in the presence of the holy angels and of the Lamb. 11 And the smoke of their torment rises forever and ever. Day and night there is no rest for those who worship the beast and its image, or for anyone who receives the mark of its name." 12 Here is a call for the perseverance of the saints who keep the commandments of God and the faith of Jesus." **-Revelation 14:9-12 BSB**

A WORLDWIDE RESET IS COMING. ARE YOU READY?

SALVATION

Salvation is only through faith in Jesus Christ

"21 But now, apart from the law, the righteousness of God has been revealed, as attested by the Law and the Prophets. 22 And this righteousness from God comes through faith in Jesus Christ to all who believe. There is no distinction, 23 for all have sinned and fall short of the glory of God, 24 and are justified freely by His grace through the redemption that is in Christ Jesus.

25 God presented Him as the atoning sacrifice through faith in His blood, in order to demonstrate His righteousness, because in His forbearance He had passed over the sins committed beforehand. 26 He did this to demonstrate His righteousness at the present time, so as to be just and to justify the one who has faith in Jesus."
-Romans 3:21-26 BSB

- **How does a person obtain eternal life?**
- **Why did Jesus have to die on the cross for our sins?**
- **Why can't our works be good enough to make it into heaven?**

THESE QUESTIONS WILL BE ANSWERED THROUGH VERSE BY VERSE EXPLANATION OF ROMANS 3:21-26.

"21 But now, apart from the law, the righteousness of God has been revealed, as attested by the Law and the Prophets."

The Law could not and did not reveal the righteousness of God that we see in Jesus Christ. The Law was to show us how short we fall to God's standards. It cannot acquit us of our shortcomings. The Law and the prophets pointed to the Messiah's sacrifice through the sacrificial system of animals.

"22 And this righteousness from God comes through faith in Jesus Christ to all who believe. There is no distinction,"

God's righteousness is obtained through Jesus' merit, not ours. He lived a sinless life by obeying God's commands (the Law). When one puts their faith in Jesus, His righteousness gets added to their account.

"23 for all have sinned and fall short of the glory of God,"

We are born in sin and are guilty even in our mother's womb. Our sins are like dirty rags, and filthy rags cause things to get worse.

"Surely I was brought forth in iniquity; I was sinful when my mother conceived me." **-Psalm 51:5 BSB**

"Each of us has become like something unclean, and all our righteous acts are like filthy rags; we all wither like a leaf, and our iniquities carry us away like the wind." **-Isaiah 64:6 BSB**

"24 and are justified freely by His grace through the redemption that is in Christ Jesus."

We are considered righteous through Jesus' favor (something we didn't deserve), in which He took our punishment upon Himself by being scourged and dying on the cross. Jesus didn't have to die for us, but His love compelled Him.

"4 Surely He took on our infirmities and carried our sorrows; yet we considered Him stricken by God, struck down and afflicted. 5 But He was pierced for our transgressions, He was crushed for our iniquities; the punishment that brought us peace was upon Him, and by His stripes we are healed." **-Isaiah 53:4-5 BSB**

"6 For at just the right time, while we were still powerless, Christ died for the ungodly. 7 Very rarely will anyone die for a righteous man, though for a good man someone might possibly dare to die. 8 But God proves His love for us in this: While we were still sinners, Christ died for us." **-Romans 5:6-8 BSB**

"25 God presented Him as the atoning sacrifice through faith in His blood, in order to demonstrate His righteousness, because in His forbearance He had passed over the sins committed beforehand."

Propitiation is something that satisfies God's wrath. God in His justice has to punish sin. Jesus presented Himself as our sacrifice and took the wrath of God for us so that we don't have to die in our sins if we accept what He did for us through faith. All the sins of the saints that lived before Christ were also placed on the cross.

"26 He did this to demonstrate His righteousness at the present time, so as to be just and to justify the one who has faith in Jesus."

God's righteousness is demonstrated in His justice of condemning and punishing sin through the death, burial, and resurrection of His Son, Jesus Christ.

Whoever places their trust and faith in Jesus Christ and believes that He died for us and rose from the grave on the third day will have everlasting life.

"16 For God so loved the world that He gave His one and only Son, that everyone who believes in Him shall not perish but have eternal life. 17 For God did not send His Son into the world to condemn the world, but to save the world through Him. 18 Whoever believes in Him is not condemned, but whoever does not believe has already been condemned, because he has not believed in the name of God's one and only Son." **-John 3:16-18 BSB**

88.
NOTES

1.

2.

3.

4.

5.

6.

7.

8.

9.

10.

89.
NOTES

1.

2.

3.

4.

5.

6.

7.

8.

9.

10.

90.
NOTES

1. _____

2. _____

3. _____

4. _____

5. _____

6. _____

7. _____

8. _____

9. _____

10. _____

91.
NOTES

1.

2.

3.

4.

5.

6.

7.

8.

9.

10.

CPSIA information can be obtained
at www.ICGtesting.com
Printed in the USA
LVHW081820220622
721890LV00011B/293